Paradise Takeaway

Alistair Noon grew up in Aylesbury. He studied German and Russian at Bristol University and has lived in Berlin since the early nineties, bar a couple of years in China. His translations of the Russian poet Osip Mandelstam have appeared in the *Guardian* and *New Statesman* as well as three volumes from Shearsman Books. *Paradise Takeaway* is the third full-length collection of his own poetry.

First published in the UK in 2023 by Two Rivers Press
7 Denmark Road, Reading RG1 5PA.
www.tworiverspress.com

ISBN 978-1-915048-09-7

1 2 3 4 5 6 7 8 9

Two Rivers Press is represented in the UK by Inpress Ltd
and distributed by BookSource.

Cover illustration and design by Sally Castle
Text design by Nadja Guggi and typeset in Janson and Parisine

Printed and bound in Great Britain by Severn, Gloucester

Paradise Takeaway

Alistair Noon

By the same author

Earth Records (Nine Arches, 2012)
The Kerosene Singing (Nine Arches, 2015)
Surveyors' Riddles (with Giles Goodland, Sidekick Books, 2015)
QUAD (Longbarrow, 2017)
Two Verse Essays (Longbarrow, 2022)

Translations
Osip Mandelstam, *Concert at a Railway Station* (Shearsman, 2018)
Osip Mandelstam, *The Voronezh Workbooks* (Shearsman, 2022)
Osip Mandelstam, *Occasional and Joke Poems* (Shearsman, 2022)

Also by Two Rivers Poets

David Attwooll, *The Sound Ladder* (2015)
Charles Baudelaire, *Paris Scenes* translated by Ian Brinton (2021)
William Bedford, *The Dancers of Colbek* (2020)
Kate Behrens, *Man with Bombe Alaska* (2016)
Kate Behrens, *Penumbra* (2019)
Kate Behrens, *Transitional Spaces* (2022)
Conor Carville, *English Martyrs* (2019)
David Cooke, *A Murmuration* (2015)
David Cooke, *Sicilian Elephants* (2021)
Tim Dooley, *Discoveries* (2022)
Jane Draycott, *Tideway* (re-issued 2022)
Jane Draycott & Lesley Saunders, *Christina the Astonishing* (re-issued 2022)
Claire Dyer, *Interference Effects* (2016)
Claire Dyer, *Yield* (2021)
John Froy, *Sandpaper & Seahorses* (2018)
James Harpur, *The Examined Life* (2021)
Maria Teresa Horta, *Point of Honour* translated by Lesley Saunders (2019)
Ian House, *Just a Moment* (2020)
Philippe Jaccottet, *In Winter Light* translated by Tim Dooley (2022)
Rosie Jackson & Graham Burchell, *Two Girls and a Beehive* (2020)
Rosie Jackson, *Love Leans over the Table* (2023)
Gill Learner, *Chill Factor* (2016)
Gill Learner, *Change* (2021)

Sue Leigh, *Chosen Hill* (2018)
Sue Leigh, *Her Orchards* (2021)
Becci Louise, *Octopus Medicine* (2017)
Mairi MacInnes, *Amazing Memories of Childhood, etc.* (2016)
Steven Matthews, *On Magnetism* (2017)
Steven Matthews, *Some Other Where* (2023)
Henri Michaux, *Storms under the Skin* translated by Jane Draycott (2017)
Kate Noakes, *Goldhawk Road* (2023)
René Noyau, *Earth on Fire and other Poems* translated by Gérard Noyau with Peter Pegnall (2021)
James Peake, *Reaction Time of Glass* (2019)
James Peake, *The Star in the Branches* (2022)
Peter Robinson & David Inshaw, *Bonjour Mr Inshaw* (2020)
Peter Robinson, *English Nettles* (re-issued 2022)
Peter Robinson, *Retrieved Attachments* (2023)
Lesley Saunders, *Nominy-Dominy* (2018)
Lesley Saunders, *This Thing of Blood & Love* (2022)
Jack Thacker, *Handling* (2018)
Robin Thomas, *The Weather on the Moon* (2022)
Susan Utting, *Half the Human Race* (2017)
Jean Watkins, *Precarious Lives* (2018)

And as my feet approached the border,
I sensed a strengthening grip
across my chest, I think my eyes
were even starting to drip.

— Heinrich Heine, 'Germany: A Winter's Tale' (1844)

I.

In which our hero lands at Luton Airport

I seem to preserve a certain loyalty
to the Flying House of Orange
as the pressure sticks its thumbs in my lugs
and I suck my herbal lozenge.

The silence through the oval window –
a blue room pierced by a lamp.
Inside the homing, humming tube
my legs lock into cramp.

I see you wedged at the end of my row,
your ears plugged into flight mode,
and Bertolt Brecht on the seat between us.
My laptop's shut and stowed.

From the cloudy peaks and plains in the sun,
I can feel the photon gain.
Beneath us now, the climate cuts,
the austere, sporadic rain,

and below this travelling superstructure
the rippling, Brownian motion
of stacked containers pinned across
the trading, trawling ocean.

This North Sea flight is short, so no,
I won't be grabbing my share
of scratchcards so one sole investor
can land as a millionaire

when a re-education lecture calls
from speakers high in the air.
And while this orange ferry unloads,
there'll be no brassy fanfare,

no heavenly lyres or village bands
or all-male valley choirs
will greet the wings of this great gull
as they flap the shores of the shires,

begin their approach to my socialization,
start their descent to my genes,
fly over the schools I grew from, zygote
of my folks' economic means.

Since physicists made principles
uncertain, no sod knows
which way the photon's going to veer
if you know how fast it goes,

and no one knows the rate it moves at,
given the route it swerves.
The words I push and pull disturb
the object I observes.

But though the models flip direction,
and every trip's short-haul,
I feel I know which way an Airbus
319 would fall

should theory fail and practice be
a field five miles from Luton:
on Earth, it's usually fine to trust
the laws of Isaac Newton

as we knife the low, migrating clouds,
sheets bulging with water,
the land's unstable, hoisted ceiling.
I only recall the border

between the changing states of airspace
when the landing gear unfurls,
ailerons pop up like zombies, the double
bump of the arse as the wheels

skid for a moment. We skim to a stop.
Toy lighthouses flash their amber.
Two dayglo suits who haul our bags
out of the hold will clamber

onto the belts where sleek components
take tours around the planet,
the handlers' job not to make the machine
but only now to man it,

their ears under plastic diadems.
And like some pharaoh at Karnak
I breeze the stairs and fail to kiss
the raindrop-gritted tarmac,

then slam through doors, peg it up escalators,
down corridors, flights and lifts,
past signs to bogs and bags and read
the immigration hieroglyphs.

I make my call in the terminal building,
then head for the test of entry
to flip up the photo fit to show
I can buy my round in this country,

can gather more data about my folks,
work hard as a real-ale tester,
rant at a London graveyard and
the literary scene of Leicester –

an eye on the time, my tum and the bus
low-chugging away in its bay:
the 61 will take me to Aylesbury,
not stopping at Paradise Takeaway.

II.

A case of mistaken identity

UK/EU. All Other. The border
had forced us into our factions,
but too few staff were on duty that day,
due to industrial action.

The retractable cordons turned and reversed
to handle the human freight;
there were signs of up to how many minutes
that baggage was having to wait.

The constant channels of spawning arrivals
meandered their route to the sea
and into a sluggish, manmade delta,
a port at the end of each tributary.

I stepped across the thick white line
to get my mirrorbook checked,
but somehow mixed it up with my
One Hundred Poems of Brecht.

I held those pages up for inspection,
open some unknown place.
The Lady of Passport Control peered down
and up and into my face.

"*Bertolt Brecht.* I have to say,"
she sighed, "I'm one of your sceptics:
I must admit I'm not so keen on
In Praise of Dialectics.

I know you try your best to take
the stance of the labouring poor
and those below. But that ain't easy
when you're a kind of have-more.

It isn't wrong to have been born
the son of one who bossed
an assembly line about, but time
has a lower unit cost.

And though your ballads rattle at
the bankers' fiscal fetters,
it tires my eyes to always have it
YELLED OUT IN CAPITAL LETTERS.

So you can free yourselves, you told us
without so much as a blink,
you'll have to think for yourselves, and left
a list of things to think.

In every verse I sense you've read
the Apostles and the Prophets:
it seems your sermon's often true,
is true but seldom honest.

Yes, some is true and some is not
and some might even be fine.
I grew up as the son of well-off folks –
yes, that's an honest line.

Forgive me for saying that I prefer
your poem about Cortés,
whose men pitched camp in a sunlit meadow
one evening, line three says.

They spark their fires and toast their meat,
get pissed beneath the stars,
but as they wake, they find themselves
fenced in by wooden bars.

Their axes in stumps outside the ring
of growth, the detainees try
to snap the twining branches but soon
they can only guess the sky,

as the jungle grows and groans and twists,
trussing them up with its threads,
and they die, exhausted, the trees around
and between them and over their heads.

I think that one was kind of honest,
even if it wasn't true."
She flashed her eyes, slid back my book,
and I proceeded through.

III.

In which he reflects upon the nutritional habits
of his countrypeople, and his own

At Luton Arrivals I looked about
at Pret-A-Put-On-Weight,
The Body Mass Shop and Burger Thing:
my mouth swam up to the bait.

"The 61" I thought "can wait..."
And so did a flickering flicker
of pixels halting a synching screen
as I gazed at the constant ticker

that crawled below it... +++ *Such a waistline*
the world had never seen,
an ever-turning, plump equator
right where their ships had been +++

The pixels flickered, and I saw shapes:
red-costumed men in fields
helping banana farmers boost
their cotton export yields

or send their surplus grain to works
where piston wheels would spin
and bells would bugle-call the time
to down your nosh from a tin

with salt and sugar for speed. +++ *As if*
stocked up with metal jars,
Scotts en route to the Pole, they made
their dinners like their cars +++

The town pigged out although the soil
they ploughed was somewhere else,
the calories and convenience now
stacked up on Tesco shelves +++

Yes, there it was, my college of food!
My culinary alma maters
and gastrotutors – burgers and whoppers,
hot bangers and chipolatas!

+++ *The klaxon honked with cancer stats,*
heart attacks, TV *panic;*
their scales revealed the national diet
was one nutritional Titanic +++

The pixels formed five portioned lifeboats
named after various veg,
with shivering figures watching pedometers
right at the cardiac edge

in sight of the doomed on their adipose ship,
where the band struck up a recipe,
and as they sank honked out the theme
of the new nutritional therapy

across the liner's sinking screens,
where Captain Oliver manhandles
a pan to channel cooking with olives
while watching cooking channels.

+++ *Across those daytime talking screens,*
they watched celebrity police
actioning salt and sugar and fat
on behalf of the freshly obese +++

They had become another nation,
from Shetland down to Cornwall,
a fish in the mouth from Fishguard to Yarmouth,
convinced it's totally normal

and totally Great +++ Such a waistline
the world had never seen,
an ever-turning, plump equator
right where their ships had been +++ …

"Sod that," I thought, as the signal returned,
"we've known since M. Foucault
that every Power snack states how much
our fat reserves should grow.

The fitness studio? That's for the idle.
We've known since Aristotle
it's when we've got no quicker pleasure
that we hit the crisps and the bottle."

I looked about the limited offers,
the burgers with free desserts,
the air-conditioned grins of the staff
and the constant calorie alerts.

I looked along the lamp-lit counters,
lighthouses lining a coastline,
while waiting for my fries, looked down
at that waistline, and it was mine.

IV.

In which he encounters certain changes in Luton's bus network negatively impacting his journey to Aylesbury

On the airport concourse, I saw the truth:
THERE WAS NO 61.
Not since last week. Oh no. Oh fuck.
My ride for a fiver had gone

like a bat in the dusk. That glittering city's
bus-roosts had been rearranged,
and shuttles now left, like hopper flights,
for Luton Interchange.

Via the Interchange busways swooped
to guide me eitherway home,
the place I couldn't go now by
one single route alone.

How long would I hang around that place
where all the buslines meet,
of blustery gusts, a phone booth (bust)
and the shelter's splintered seat,

of stops and starts and scrupulous queues,
of dull, expected delays
determined down to the minute by
the daisy dot displays,

and times that arrive without a bus,
although we know they're running?
Maybe I'd missed one. There was a sign.
Messiah, it said, was coming.

In the middle of their shift, oh would
the bar staff take my note
and let me home to the top front seats,
dawdling the Aylesbury road,

and nest in that panoramic lounge...?
It wasn't strange it was strange
when the capless pilot answered "Cheers"
while tapping out my change,

the coins like kids in trunks down a chute
at Luton's Galaxy Leisure,
those junior natural Epicureans,
experts in practical pleasure.

I'd made it all the way to the top,
to the front where my regular seats are,
the mobile first-floor glass around me,
with a slice of last night's pizza.

The 61 twitched from its hibernation,
flapped out of its dimlit bay,
en route to Aylesbury's seventies bus-cave
and into the dusking day,

past swept-back wings that pointed to Letchworth,
Stevenage and Hitchen –
recorded a near-miss event with a navi-
gationally challenged pigeon –

across the junctions under the jets
and past the blinking lights of delay,
and the white-gloss front and red-fonted sign,
to our left, of Paradise Takeaway.

V.

A brief memoir of flying with British Airways

It vanished behind us. I thought of the time
before we'd got shot of the ground
and I'd met the eyes of a cabin crew
whose souls were Heathrow-bound.

The runway already pollocked with rain,
I ignored their professional smile
as I jerked my head like a robot bride
along the light-hyphened aisle

and tried front crawl to squeeze to my seat
and settle my black-jeaned arse
into the plush, blue-belted cradle
of BA Economy Class.

The in-flight mag, the accident card
and puke bag – all in good order.
Before me, a thick red curtain recalled
a gate at a fortified border,

as if that imperious cloth might drape
a tribal tabernacle.
I clunked my belt to the theme of packets
of peanuts beginning to crackle.

The blue-scarf border force strode right through
but left a chink where I saw
the flapping headlines and balding heads
who'd boarded by the front door.

The curtain parted: a trolley and one
high-altitude butler for hire.
"If anyone wants one, we have some papers
that First Class do not require."

I held out my hands but not to a truck
flinging out sacks of beans,
unfurled those great white wings and found
world news on page thirteen:

cockpits in battle and cabins at peace,
the holds beginning to shift –
it was all as quick as the spin of a photon
and slow as an oilslick's drift.

When coffee was served I elected to take it
enthroned in my middle seat.
Dabbing my lips, I surveyed the ranks,
and sipped, and wiggled my feet.

And so I ruffled those great white feathers.
Where had exchange rates gone?
I scanned Commodities, then flipped back
to the royal arse on page one...

VI.

The journey to Aylesbury. He procures a pint of real ale and reflects on Aylesbury's role in the English Civil War

The bluetoothed roadies on parcel rounds,
and out in their aprons, the farmers,
the stock star drives and rockbroker barns,
a paddock of local llamas,

the empty bus-stop benches, the separate
bins of the village Greens...
In our holding patterns around estates,
we jousted approaching windscreens:

the 61 did its *do-si-do*
round awkward cars, our chauffeur
accelerated straight at a mound of leaves,
then performed a *pas de deux* –

bang on the window what the
a branch, as if some arse
had delivered a stone like a scrap of Skylab
to the bus's plexiglass.

We barged aside that scratching claw,
cruised past more teenage haunts,
the pubs where no one sits, revived
as fully-reserved Thai restaurants.

We swung into Aylesbury late that night,
the inner ring road rumbling,
as was my stomach again: my taste buds
homed in on Hong Kong dumpling.

I recall the final, croaking words
that salty won-ton said:
"Master, get me a pint of real ale!"
and we headed straight down the King's Head,

the *Eschenbräu* of Aylesbury Vale,
with its blossoms of Beechwood Bitter,
Three Hundreds Old and Chiltern Ale
that deserve a decent Twitter,

a pub that put up Hangman Jeffreys,
where Harry pulled Ann Boleyn –
I tested my head, then texted back
my queen in flat Berlin.

They even put up the Grim Protector,
whose men would Battle-of-Brill
the Oxford Royalists. Centuries later,
they re-enact it still

without the killing, though with some bruises,
this foray that signalled a draw
that's still in force, when the King's men sparked
the smoke with a flint to the straw.

VII.

A treatise on the statues on the Market Square in Aylesbury, and their political significance

At the top of the Market Square, John Hampden
refused to cough up for ships
and now points out like Peter the Great,
well crimped and with firm lips.

His cough has gone, his boots of bronze
are still: no breastplate breathes.
At this kingless Parliamentarian's plinth,
the viscounts drop off wreaths.

He points across to a later MP
in metal, who made PM,
the chef whose dishes the Michelin critics
of history praise and condemn,

who made his Queen the Empress of Spice.
Head Cook of the House, Disraeli
passed housing laws, the man no Lords
dumped before the Old Bailey

when freight was drowning crews by the day,
and he holed the Commons votes
on cargo loading lines because
the MPs all owned boats.

Down at the County Hall, Charles Compton,
Edwardian major general,
a Baron of Chesham and Master of Buckhounds,
awarded his place on a pedestal,

Inspector of Yeomanry hunting the cobbles
in his riding boots and crop,
tachetastic looks across that veldt
to a diamond-mine-stocked shop.

All on! I walked out into the night
beneath the County Clock.
The Lantern was dark. The Swan asleep.
The Ship was in dry dock.

Across the square The Bell was silent,
the Three Pigeons had long since flown,
and I wondered how many drunks had lunged
across those cobblestones

where farmers sold their walking steaks
and toasted rosettes and prizes,
and those who'd stolen gold or bread
woke up before the Assizes.

Certainly you, John Wilkes, once known
as the ugliest man in the land,
devoted, we know, to his only daughter,
a father of five, unplanned,

incendiary pamphleteer, one more
new member for Aylesbury ducks,
who brought a baboon to the Hellfire Club
and made High Sheriff of Bucks,

who libelled the king, defended the liberty
of printers yelling disquiet
at royal expenses, and later sent in
the rifles to fire on a riot.

Perhaps of a day you'd wander about
the market, among the eggs
and local ham and loaves, big cheese,
a pig up on its hind legs.

Ugliest man in the land, is that
why all you've got is a plaque?
Disraeli and Hampden point and stare
from the front, the side and the back.

And where's Nat Rothschild, who had the manors
to hold the City in fealty
and bumped his way from house to House,
where he too sat for Aylesbury?

Nor's there a sign on the Market Square
of Joseph Stalin's candidate
who got caught up one by-election
in a brutally frank debate

with Brylcreemed gents in suits who showed him
the Aylesbury cobbles, each
as far as a candidate's nasal bone
can land, on these rocks, from a beach.

VIII.

He gets home and tries to make a piece of toast
with his favourite yeast extract

My ancestral home. The lights were out.
And deep and dark inside me
I sensed a deeper, darker sense,
an ancient poet to guide me

down through the shelves. That Chiltern Ale
had roused the munchies, admit it,
you greedy sod. But what was this?
My folks' new kitchen, fitted

after forty years, now left me flailing
and falling, ready to drown:
shifting and shutting the covert cupboards,
my appetite foraged around.

I floundered about, found Branston Pickle
where there used to be Bran Flakes.
My elbow almost bunker-busted
two secret Dundee cakes.

As when a Windows version rolls out
and you know the commands are there
but not where they were, and the admin's not
on call to tell you where,

I scanned displays, the tool and taskbars,
for toaster, knife and plate,
the butter and bread. And now I went
prospecting for that black agate

I crave and praise, the glassy prize
some know is a national jewel
more vital to our survival than
three months' aviation fuel,

while taste-deniers like Paul Cooke
would rather be force-fed drips
of industrial solvent or Brent Crude
than let it pollute their lips.

Ah there it was, the screen-black housing,
its software good to install.
I revolved the jar in my hand like a slightly
wonky snooker ball.

Give us this day our daily toast
with a dollop of Marmite. Amen!
The crust was crisp, the butter oozed.
I was ready to lick that gem,

that salty sludge, its dripping darkness –
oh how long I'd lacked it! –
that Paul would seal in a nuclear vault,
but I would always extract its

exquisite dregs from the Gallic glass,
whose tang was first released
by a Hessian chemist one night messing
about with brewer's yeast.

When the matter's gone, conserve the energy:
what's civilized and nice is
to rinse the jar for a veggie stock,
then stock it with herbs and spices.

"That's my idea! You got something round
your mouth." From halfway down
the Marmite-dark stairs, the stair-lift whirred
with my dad in his dressing gown.

IX.

He watches telly

The living room dim as *Nostromo*'s hold,
I'd garrisoned crisps and pint
on the coffee table, my toes were up,
the remote control was mine.

A spot on the screen. In seconds, a cosmos
exploded in science fiction,
the Earth a jewel in the claw of the Tribbians,
those croakers with RP diction.

They look like us, although they wear
strange hair upon their faces.
And no one knows from where they've warp-jumped,
what ancient, cloud-wigged places.

They stand behind enormous zap guns
and say their planet is green.
We learn they've landed on primitive worlds
and that they're ruled by a queen.

Some they've crushed and some cajoled,
some they shove or bribe.
Some they name a local world,
and some they call a space-tribe.

Some pay Tribute, some do trade
or slave away while ill,
some eat their fill while others starve,
and some they simply kill.

Some of their planets are like bright cities
or else a market town,
some a village on which five hundred
suns will never go down.

Then there attack the N'zisA,
an empire nastier than theirs.
The Tribbians tacevac some worlds,
then win back all their shares.

The imperial planets grumble and grouch,
and most of them rebel,
but come and dance when great galactic
tea parties get held,

and the Tribbians source their rocks again
from the Human Republic of Earth
at prices economists feel are fair
and less than the rocks are worth.

When tea-dancers fluff steps, the Tribs
will flog resourceful nations
phasers to emphasize their friendship
and strong bilateral relations.

On and on and on they trib
about the War they won,
and find no time to comment on
the extortion schemes they'd run

for all the zapships zapping across
their dark galactic screens
to zap the Satanic N'zisA
to galactic smithereens.

Respected Tribbian historians write
it was all a treat for space-trade –
they set the rules, they set the routes
(although mistakes were made) –

and blurb each other's books in which
the old imperial masters,
with mays and mights, althoughs, perhapses,
incurred imperial disasters,

and wispy-headed planetary officers
sit in their leafy gardens
to tell the telly they saved the Earth
and never once thought of a pardon.

In fantasy novels those Tribsters tell
themselves they're cosmic hobbits,
although they ruled each planet from
the icecaps down to the tropics.

The Tribbians. I remembered the show
from when I was five years old.
I yawned, and obliterated the cosmos
as the BBC credits unrolled.

"Are you still up?" my dad called down,
as I tip-toed the last of the bends
in the stairs and fumbled my book of utopias.
"You're burning the candle at both ends..."

X.

Breakfast, and a trip to the DVD Exchange, prompting reflections on a long-running BBC TV science fiction series

"He lives. Good morning!" Around the kitchen
my mum was clanking the plates.
"There's tea in the pot. I've put on the toast.
There's All-Bran but no Bran Flakes."

In the room, the Band of the Royal Marines
on BBC *Breakfast* gave
the munching, crunching, slurping nation
"A Life on the Ocean Wave".

I was happy to taste the toast of home,
but needed a dose of air.
I downed my tea, lashed up my mac,
and followed the closest thoroughfare

towards the High Street's heap of rocks
for my usual, crucial shop
when I row to the TV Channel Islands
to gather my annual crop

of mussels ripped from the recent past,
a cheap and glittering harvest...
It isn't hard to travel in time
when you own your very own Tardis.

The DVD player's my time machine
to travel to times I've missed,
new series old mates are gabbing about,
or at least their jokes and gist.

The disc will click into place and whirr,
like a Tardis core, to the truth
of bosses and bossed there is in *The Office*,
the oosh in the *The Mighty Boosh.*

Or else I tap disorderly coordinates
to whirl me back to the seventies
where side-burned cops in bad suits would screech
through Manchesters, Leeds and Coventries,

where Paradise laid its towel in Spain,
and a being called Freddie Laker
was first to flog no-frills to the States,
and *Doctor Who* was Tom Baker,

eccentric gentleman native-saver
who never quite gets away
from those impartial, imperial officials,
the Time Lords of Gallifrey,

in the episodes made of silverfoil
and a comedy Chinese gang
whose made-up boss had dubious eyes
in *The Talons of Wen Chiang.*

They all got zapped by the dragon too,
and before the tunnelling theme
the female's tasks were chiefly to ask
and listen, screw up and scream.

The baddies aren't always *Wen Chiang* now.
Perhaps the screams have got less?
We may permit ourselves a brief
parsec to cheer on progress,

but the DVD is still in the slot
to forward or to rewind,
and we travel through time at the very same time,
both ahead, it seems, and behind.

Forward I'll go and back I went,
I zap to the audio commentary
both on the disc and live on the couch
as my girlfriend gets derogatory.

Forward I went and back I'll go
to my favourite bits. I switch
to Specials for how the Krynoids were made,
the way Tom's scarf was stitched,

the heads of stars who travelled the stars,
and the jovial Terence Dicks,
humanoid trapped in a skew toupee,
wecalling the seventies scwipts.

Clips of a future filmed in the past
spin by before me. Splendid.
I watch them once. For most of the actors,
the episode has ended.

Forward I go and there I look
into that overweight hole
that pigs out on light, then back I went
and tapped the remote control.

So I rose with a pile of discs
and strode to the till to pay,
each brick in the pedestrian zone
paving the pigeon's way.

XI.

He takes the train into London

Where buskers mete out New Model Army
to risk my musical asbos,
and the Odeon where I gasped at *Star Wars*
was boarded up due to asbestos,

I'd passed the temple of hot cross-trainers
for those who'd like to be fatless;
the bridge to the rising car park, roof
to blankets and one bare mattress.

My back to Disraeli, Hampden and Wilkes
the King's Head, the Battle of Brill,
my folks and the DVD Exchange,
I saw far-seeing Coombe Hill

that prevails across the Vale of Aylesbury:
a model easyJet soars
above the obelisk which enlists
the farmers killed by Boers.

I was stuck in a chugging Bounty Bar,
a blue-and-white packet of trekkers.
Rockbrokers lurk near stock stars here
where the line runs close to Chequers,

and on this rock where waves do stage-dives
from Caithness down to Kent,
the rich have never been far from the poor,
investment far from its rent,

liquidity treated, pumped and run
into homes; though at its source it's
the same in taste, it splutters out here
through separate hot and cold faucets.

As when Dante circled in circles
or a Skylab's orbit decays,
the enormous mass of central London
pulls in the ferrous railways

honking the cuttings, detached estates,
the avenues, crescents and rows:
consultants on cancer and annual results
scurry back here to their burrows,

passing through woods on a blowy evening
from rain-pecked station car parks.
Alongside the Neasden Depot sidings
we sidled, the rails wept sparks.

Onwards we passed the rumbling gardens,
the semicircles of semis,
slipped under bridges where cameras catch
the locals looking for empties,

to glimpse kebab-shopped Victorian streets,
the monuments of council flats,
their vertical stairwells dotting the distance
like lit-up industrial vats,

plunged into the tunnel that guides us under
the homes where nobody's home,
to emerge under arches and surge for the barriers
at long-platformed Marylebone.

XII.

The South Bank. He has a Vision of Total Surveillance

Traipsing along the dank South Bank
where the grainy granite stems
the flood and flow, the swirl and swill
of that old delinquent, the Thames,

and the cavalry charges on Waterloo Bridge
outflank the Festival Hall,
where cooks and crooks and ex-prime ministers
grin at you out of the stalls,

I surveyed the river, observed the crowd,
zoomed in on a section of sky.
All the way up to the seamless clouds,
there climbed the London Eye.

Not the revolving panopticon
where visitors popped into pods
will go for a spin for thirty quid,
live half-an-hour as the gods.

No, this was London Eye version 2.0,
on its bolted-down steel pole,
growth-hormoned beanstalk rising up
and under remote control.

It stood there rising on and up
like one of those redwood trees,
with a hundred eyes that peered around
three hundred and ninety degrees.

Far up, up there, up there at the top
was a coral of stony cameras,
elbows practising jerky salutes,
about-turning to new panoramas.

Those eyes were shooting a documentary,
the daily trek of the traffic
around the dark M25,
for the National Geographic.

Their gaze retraced its way so they
could see who'd punched that dent
in a Luton phone and who was doing
a bunk in Stoke-on-Trent,

and at the very same time they roved
across South London's flats,
the Downs and Dover, over the Channel,
to Calais, yea to Sangatte.

Rumour had it that on bright days
that cinematic Medusa
could even see across the Alps
and the Med to Lampedusa.

And working along that insect eye,
with luck, you could see a cradle
that hung on a thread, up hard against
the windows flooding that temple

to vision and visibility. Up there
was a bloke with a cloth and sponge
washing and polishing, rubbing away
at spots of aerial gunge.

Even at night he'd be there wiping
and squeezing as warning lights
made wolf eyes aimed at twenty airports'
non-stop incoming flights.

Down at the base of that great pole
by London's miniature Yangtze,
there hung one final old-style camera
stencilled on by Banksy

(they'd caught him on camera, of course). It too
focussed its eye on the nation,
beside a small blue sign that read
CCTV IN OPERATION.

XIII.

He explores the financial district of London referred to as The City

Then I loitered across the Millennium Bridge
and back to another millennium,
when walkers were walking across and the bridge
wobbled in fright, a phenomenon

I had often noticed: our steps were linking us
into one huge oscillation,
and we felt our feet increase the synchronous
lateral excitation,

like traders trading the moves of traders.
I headed past St. Paul's,
the Pret a Mangers for deregulated pigeons
where once there had been City walls,

towards the glassy Towers of London,
where top-fermenting bosses
bubble away at the tops of their vats
that brew up gains and losses,

saying "Without Yeast hath no man Beer
for the Wort will not budge,
and without Yeast hath no man Bread,
and the Marmite stayeth in the sludge",

on in the rain and over the paving
where Romans wandered their forum,
and Lloyd's take ships and Keith Richards' fingers
to underwrite and insure them.

Inside that tower's spiral binding,
the lifts and ducts outsourced,
three centuries of silent clerks
have pored over loss reports

beneath Marine & Offshore, below
the Lutine Bell that told
of cargo lost, a gong from a ship
that sank with its burgled gold.

And over the scribes who write the bitterest
and truest songs of seafaring
hangs War, Terrorism and Political Violence.
But over at Barclays and Barings

the *force majeure* of lunch had struck,
and the skirts and suits in the Gherkin
were knocking off for an offering of crisps
and a pint in the Stock and Firkin.

The Glass Carrot too, its cross-slit spire
now peckish; the Aubergine,
where derivatives bounce about the planet
like hounds on a trampoline,

where the stressed minds of a generation
will knock up special deals
on exotic dishes with novel ingredients
the menus never reveal;

the Twin Courgettes that serve junk debt
and the share-backed pension plan,
where the song they hum on the trading desk
is *Je ne regrette rien.*

My eyes unpeeled the Bendy Banana,
where ripening fruit's short-sold,
and asset strippers cream banana
splits as factories fold.

The City was lunching on wages again:
among those high headquarters
I took my seat while staff took on
a Soviet harvest of orders,

some of the diners willing to wait,
some wishing their sushi *now.*
As long as the dishes landed on time,
it didn't much matter how.

XIV.

He visits a North London cemetery, where he is in turn visited by a well-known political philosopher. German accent

I headed for Highgate's ivy sepulchres,
where death still has some legroom.
I wandered along the leafy paths
to a grey and granite tomb.

"Ah zere you are," said a voice. "You'ff come
from ze lant vot I used to know.
Tell me my frient from ze continent's centre,
is ze *Kommune* on ze go?

Here vere I'm stuck, some haff got fatter
and uzzers are still in zeir fettas.
Tell me, oh trafller betveen zese lants,
is it in Germany betta?

Haff ze vorkers understoot ze true nature
of ze manufakturt *Artikel*?
Haff zey begun to behafe like a vave
or is each of zem a *Partikel*?

A frient of mine, a Comrate Heine,
whose vorks might be among
the vones you'ff read I sink vonce said
Ve need a betta song."

"The Russians rose but the rest of the world
didn't rise up in their entirety.
The places that did, they ended up
all state and no society.

The Dictatorship of the Proletariat,
comrade, I regret to report,
got stuck at the stage of dictatorship,
didn't wither away as it ought."

"Vell vell," he said, "zat's very strange.
At least ze ret flak vas unfurlt.
Tell me vat happent zough, iff you please,
in ze rest of ze industrializt vorlt?"

"Since relocating into the grave,
you may not have heard the gunfire,
the gravestone-dropping planes in a war
against the Evillest Empire.

The diggers of death then stopped for breath,
there began a different boom:
there were lots of lots to rebuild and rent,
and out of the terraced gloom

came cleaner air and towers with views
where few now knew their neighbours,
and grids and grants and garden cities,
and better pay for their labours."

"*Nein nein nein nein nein nein nein*!
How coult my seory be rong?
Herr Heine vas not out of key
ven he sang *Ve need a new song*!"

"You saw the villagers leave their wheels
to crowd the shuttling looms,
and thought that as machines made more
and the cycles of busts and booms

spun on and on and faster and deeper
they'd start to forget their skills,
their paths would merge, and the working class
would then zone in for the kill.

But the contradictions didn't quite grow
the way you wrote they would –
enough got rich enough that the plebs
seemed to have split for good.

Some picked up phones, some made the phones,
and some poured tar onto roads
or sweated their lives in the cotton zones,
and some wrote programming codes.

And some poured tea for easyJet
while some poured gin for BA
(yes how they relate to the means of production's
the same at the end of the day)."

"Whose vork is it vot makes ze goods?
Zat's the vorking *Klasse*, is it not?
In Tooting, Wedding or Timbuktu
or on ze Moon, *mein Gott!*"

"Calm down, *mein Herr*, this could be a case
of a tower on a hill that can't
quite tell the finger where we are
but only where we aren't.

The profits thinned, and the State went on
a diet with some of its prices
so spots for lunch could stay the same,
despite the Oil Crisis.

That wealth will flow like a petrocarbon's
really a bit of a fib:
the capital's towers don't get up and walk,
there's dosh for a dome or a warship.

Now one band sings about planets and moons,
another about space-time.
One track's about our jobs and shops,
another about the sub-prime."

"I see," he said. "But all ze same,
I'm sure ze *Krisis* grows."
"Too right," I said. "All right," he said,
"then vot do you propose?

For if you vont to find a vay
to abolish priority boardink,
yong mann, you'll haff to find a vay
to halt ze profit hoardink."

"You know that mane and beard of yours
are a wig on a granite block?
They took your head and hammered your thoughts
into that cemetery rock.

And are you sure you didn't know
the things your books would bring?
Karl, go on, admit you became
Plato's philosopher king.

Although I too perhaps confuse
the galleries of my mind –
Plato's cave of its own – with all
the handprints we could find,

and it isn't nice to think the brain
a bit of a panelled club,
to say *Perhaps I'm going too fast,*
or maybe you ain't keeping up,

the only way to do what's right
is to think you're right and wrong
at least a little, although I know
that that might take too long..."

"You haff a point, yong mann, but ze speed
you neet to fly depents
on vere you look from. In intellektuell terms
you're burnink ze candle at ze bos ents."

Just at that moment, that Highgate day,
that stony bearded head
morphed into a shape all grey and plump,
its mottled wings aspread.

XV.

He recalls the privatization of the railways and his difficulties in procuring a rail ticket to Scotland

It waddled away, and I wandered off
to the techno-hit mid-nineties
when the transport grid transitioned back
to the stage of feudal societies.

I'd wanted rails to Scotland and
some legroom, once revived
with a proper brew at Victoria, where
my Berlin coach had arrived.

"Return to St. Andrews." Behind the glass,
the Blue Lady of Tickets said
"We don't sell that no more," and waved
her fair and well-brushed head.

"How so, gode mayde?" I replied, "I preye thee,
tel me, whether thou knowst,
whenne I kan gette oon?" "I'm sorry," she sighed,
"we don't serve East or West Coast."

I sauntered across to a travelle agence
that had sold such fares. "I seke
passage by iren wey. Sellest thou swylke?"
"Nah mate. Not since last week."

"Where may I gette swylke travelle, sire?"
He shunted me off to King's Cross
to queue for an hour to hear the road
to the north was going to cost

all four of my limbs. So back I rode
to where I'd arrived at Victoria,
where all I could book was an all-night coach,
and a creeping diseuphoria

revved in my mind. Six hours it took
on that day of deregulation
to regulate my solution. Something
was wrong in the equation:

I thought of Moscow three years before,
where you'd factor in three hours
at *Intourist* with its forms and phones,
and I weighed that wait against ours.

"By Goddes herte, for Cristes peyne,
fukking helle! How much of my life
do I need to obtain an off-peak return
to gette me from London to Fife?!"

"Everything all right, sir?" Two young knyghtes,
all black and blue, rose before me
beside the bays. They did not look
as if they were going to ignore me.

"No, it is not! When I needed to take
the Trans-Sib three years ago
it only took me half this time
to wangle a ticket from Moscow!

The afternoon was mine to seize
in McDonalds, the Irish Pub.
It didn't take one working day
to escape a transport hub!"

Their radio staticked. “We take it, sir,
that you wouldn’t be going so far
as to argue that we’d be best off going
back to the USSR,” –

more static-static – “the state that planned
to swap the top and the bottom,
to skip one stage, transmute a feudal
society – look where it got them.”

“At least they beat restaurants into canteens
(although mistakes were made...)
At least they had tickets to ride!” “Indeed, sir,
even those who’d rather have stayed.”

They were right, and I’d read of the recent cuts
by the Warsaw Pact and NATO
to their rolling stock. And I went and got
a cheese and coleslaw baked potato.

XVI.

He arrives at Euston

So now I saw an enormous hand
pluck people off Waterloo Bridge.
I was standing at Euston, all of the hall
infused with a starlike tinge.

The fresco switched, and strips of pepper
tumbled straight into a wok
and sizzled about, like bright canoes
splashing around a Thames dock.

I was glad the volume was down on the screen –
I was booked in the quiet zone.
Then a voice out of sync with the scene
informed us that David Jones

was needed now on the food court, and bags
could explode. "Take extra care
on slippery surfaces please", it boomed,
that soothing alto from nowhere.

High in the highest part of Departures,
one figure was flicking through
like a flipover diary: a shoal of passengers
darted their way towards Crewe,

leaving a pair of shapes in black.
Was it them? Two Twix in a packet,
they turned and murmured into their radios,
topping up air on a life jacket.

The day had come: I saw the police
could be my son or daughter.
The shock: they hadn't just got younger
but also shorter.

"What's wrong," I wanted to yell at the hall,
"with the tallest in the realm? It
seems they refuse the traffic cap,
to don the riot helmet.

Or was it ruled unfair that those
whose arm is not so long
can't help us help uphold the law,
be it right or legalized wrong?"

My platform flashed, and soon I was like
a luminous sprat, as a camera
silently spied on my part of the tank
where Jill was the duty manager.

I explored the signs on all the ways
the fishy traveller annoys,
didn't chomp my fronds or bump at the glass
or make one bubble of noise.

XVII.

Further reflections on the privatization of the railways, in the form of a Dream

Euston receded. I nodded off,
and there shimmered a uniformed spectre
along the aisle, click-clicking his puncher,
a cowled ticket inspector.

"Tickets please, all those who got on
at Sheffield or Leeds." "Excuse me,"
I growled at the darkness under the cowl,
"I'd like to see your ID."

"Certainly, sir. One sec. There you go.
That's me, the Spirit of Rail,
to whom you may submit complaints
when signals and services fail."

"Thank you," I said. "When I think of the future,
yes, there'll be a few,
so many in fact that *pars pro toto*
these few will have to do.

Why will I need a reservation
if, when I get on
the St. Pancras train at Leicester station,
my half of the train will be gone?

And why, though all the train is there,
will the platforms be too short,
so half the train must move on down
to leave by the four rear doors?

And even if there is a platform
why will I ascertain
when we creep into Cambridge that the platform
is neither side of our train?

And why, while I await announcements,
will the station staff not say
there are no wheels or bogies, coaches
G, B, H or J ?

Why does the loco speed along
at the pace of an armadillo
and the BBC make railway porn
with a thoughtful Michael Portillo?

Why will they send all Kings Cross passengers
to Finsbury Park to face
a station shut "due to crowds" that returns
"with a queuing system in place"?

Why invite me to dob in a dodger
by texting triple three
while taxes clear the project-botchers'
billion-quid debris?

Why why why why why why why
will the train have to stop half way
from London to Liverpool Lime St. because
a driver is off today?"

"Drivers today!" the passengers roared
as my voice grew hoarse and desperate.
I turned my eyes to the Spirit of Rail,
and his face was that of John Prescott.

The train had stalled in the middle of fields,
then it slowly started to chug
into a tunnel. I looked right into
that great Prescottian mug.

"We do take seriously all complaints.
Yes, it's commuter hell
in the land of Robert Stephenson
and Isambard Kingdom Brunel."

"But were things better before?" I begged,
"Speak, o Spirit of Rail!"
"Well, I can't remember the customer service,
but I'll tell you The Shunter's Tale."

XVIII.

The Spirit of Rail recalls the death of a pigeon

"In the drizzling, dieselling 1950s,
the end of the line for steam,
I was at King's Cross and scalding my lips
with the rump of the driving team

when the door banged open: Charlie the shunter.
Yeah the kettle was on the boil.
Like a stretcher, his hands held a one-eyed pigeon,
its wings near-solid with oil.

He marshalled the subject onto the table,
like some anaesthetized rabbit,
poled the feathers, uncoupled its legs.
His diagnosis: "It's had it."

We swapped our jokes and swabs of tobacco,
as Charlie wacked its neck,
but the pigeon survived that kung fu chop
and struggled about unchecked.

So Charlie pincered its neck once more
and ripped off the whole of its head
to send that aerial sailor back
to the Trafalgar Square of the dead.

I'm the Spirit of Rail, but I know my Classics.
In one of those Theban plays
Tiresias chucks a dead hawk on the flames
to divine what the State will face:

by way of cremation, Charlie slung
the pigeon slap onto the fire,
its nerves still sparking away to its muscles,
and it leapt from that firebox-pyre

to jive around the tiles of the floor,
its wings aloft and alight,
as we shifted our feet as quick as we could
and out of the way. "Oh shite,"

said Charlie, lumbering again from his seat
towards it, "watch out, mate."
He cleared the jungle, then started to stamp
and stamp at a gathering rate.

His steel-capped boots kept stamping and stamping
till the corpse stopped twitching, a mass
no longer feather, beak and claw
but blood and tissue and ash.

Then that black phoenix flew through the window
like a dried-out teabag, and Charlie
slumped down again with his lukewarm brew
and took a large bite from his sarnie."

XIX.

Our hero recalls a cross-Channel coach trip
and a dispute over fish and chips

For a second I leapt from my railway nightmare
of columbines on fire,
then dozed back off to a time before
I woke up as a frequent flyer.

For four young years I'd sought to staunch
all higher vertebrate anguish.
Nor beef nor chicken had travelled my bowels,
I'd shunned the tongue-joy of fish.

No leather, rennet or gelatine,
nor cod nor plaice nor bream.
But then a lifelong breeding pair
had returned to me in a dream.

I stood beside the galvanized steel,
by hives of buttered baps
and the battered catch beneath the striplights.
A voice said: "Open or wrapped?"

I was looking ahead to twenty-three hours
of voluntary seated pain
across the Meridian, down the Chunnel,
and over the North German Plain.

Twenty-three hours. I knew my blood
would basejump to my legs, they'd swell
into butchered pigs. Oh Bosch was wrong:
they're all sat down in Hell.

Twenty-three hours, twenty-three hours
of circulatory pain.
Why hadn't I forked out more, I thought,
for a plane or the aisle of a train?

"Open," I said. "No sorry, wrapped."
Whatever the hurt to the buttock,
at least I'd be leaving Victoria's vaults
on a fully tanked-up stomach,

as soon as I'd excavated the paper,
my fork had explored the batter...
one giant leap in dietary change,
one small step to getting fatter.

I slung on my rucksack and trotted towards
the fumes of the slumbering coach,
my jacket an amateur conjurer's cloth
across my wrapped-up catch.

"Where you goin'?" said a voice from somewhere
near Cardiff or Rhyl or Pwllheli.
"Berlin." He tagged my bag and stuffed it
into the coach's belly.

My lap was now a gourmet's table,
a nugget of cod had been chewed
when the *deus* of this *machina* called
from the front: "Someone's eatin' FOOD."

In his shirt and tie, his badge and moustache,
he banked and began his approach.
"You'll 'ave to throw it away or else
you'll just 'ave to leave this coach.

I'm sorry, I'm not 'avin' FOOD on my coach."
There were things I wanted to say:
I'll be finished soon. What's it to you?
Oh can't we just leave the UK?

But my heart and my fridge lay across the North Sea,
so I legged it out to the bin.
And as the impatient Eurocruiser
revved up, I pegged it back in.

That Moses of bags, that Noah of roads
led me, a bogus Berliner,
along three autobahns and home.
Though I was a supper thinner,

we reached the land where no company blazer
with seats to clean has to quiz you,
and the murmur waxed inside my ear:
You can't take the fish and chips with you.

XX.

He arrives in Leicester for a Poetry Reading

I opened an eye at the marches of Leicester,
the city of ring roads leading
my bristly feet along and over
and on to the evening's reading.

I settled on one of the folding chairs
that clogged that cosy hole.
As I gripped my Midlands Ale, a bearded
bard popped open a scroll.

As when a dwarf hammers your door
and demands to be let in,
I heard him homing in on the source
of all Governmental sin.

A second knock. More appalling news
barged in with the following dwarf.
Mordor, we heard, was on the move.
Then there knocked a third and a fourth,

with tales of lizards who offer awards
to the lucky dwarven poor,
while dragons keep on passing on
their hoards by dragon law.

More workers of words assailed the stage
to bewail the loss of a trove.
But by the end I knew no more
than before about Michael Gove.

On and on and on they sang
about his horrible policies.
Compared with him, Sauron himself
had certain admirable qualities.

As when the cabin pressure increases,
I heard my dad at my ear:
“What are you going to replace it with?
And how do we get there from here?”

I scribbled away: *You wield red flags*
in a world of Union Jacks
like sails amid Atlantic gales
or round Olympic tracks.

But though you know it's bad to do
your Sunday shop at Tesco
and sow petitions, too few want
to prune a manifesto

except the professionals. Govian matter
could clog the universe up.
How often does the collective need
to take a collective backrub?

Too many care but don't understand,
or understand but don't care.
Salt and vinegar make the flavour,
the toothbrush comes in pairs.

'Stalin Was Right', 'Wealth Trickles Down',
'God Save The Queen', 'Jesus Saves':
Moria names more than one maze,
and Plato has many caves.

While I was writing, a straggling dwarf,
his knobbly fingers cupped
around the mic, was starting to croak:
"All language is corrupt..."

"Give me that poem here," I cried,
and started to howl its first line,
hurled it into the microphone,
I read it, and it was mine.

XXI.

In the course of a veggie fry-up recovery breakfast, he engages in conversation with a well-known Elf and arrives at certain conclusions regarding political action

Next day, I failed to ford those ring roads
lapping the city centre.
Wherever I dipped my feet I found
no shallows to safely enter,

but along a crevice I spotted a place
called *Rivendell* that would do
tea fit for dwarves and *Gimli's Fry-Up*,
although it was well past two.

I nestled in with my phenol dose,
my appetite ferocious.
Prospecting eggs, hash browns and mushrooms,
I stared at my book of utopias.

A suit of white was hunched before me.
Each time I flipped a page,
I peeked across the top of my tome.
Slim of ear and maybe my age,

she sipped her mead and chewed her meat,
her movements a smidgeon theatrical.
I looked at her fair and flowing hair:
of course! It was Galadriel.

"Frodo," I heard her ethereal voice
from where her hair had curled,
"Frodo," she said, "there is so much
ɓqλṗ* at work in the world.

* orcshit

Those who say yes are the ones who make
and manage the permanent jobs
and decide on those who can't say no
to their two-year contracts, tops.

So many spells are praised and promised,
but only some enforced.
Consultants push through 10%,
the physios get outsourced.

Frodo, beware the management wizards
whose bonus froths away
proportionate to the sum they save
the coven on severance pay.

The employment orc reviews his career:
'I got off to a wobbly start.
But then they asked me and they tasked me
with shutting down a whole plant.'

And while a retired central banker
smiles on a floodlit stage,
fondling a mic as he savours his case
against the minimum wage,

in the foyer the hospitality staff
drill into the cork for wine,
and security guards are watching rocks
roll through the scanner's mine.

Assistant safety engineers
check timesheets and techniques:
once part of the staff, they finish careers
contractors on sixty-hour weeks.

With the click of a branded pen, physicians
shift more antibiotics,
and magic beans sprout magic beanstalks
of Giant patented profits.

Discover green tea is great for MS,
make pills to sell the doses:
this is the planet's relapsing-remitting
multiple sclerosis.

Professor Smith's invisible hand
once caught the tumbling apple,
and felt the forces upon the Earth
but not how its shine would travel.

The market that he taxonomized
was a hundred scurrying mice
and not four prowling pairs of claws
whose purrs tune into one price!

To plan a nuclear plant then talk
of energy markets appears
to split the brain when you guarantee
a price for thirty-five years."

"Oh you're so right," I spluttered my tea,
"Galadriel, what should we do?
We need a new brew, an improved brew,
for the old one has started to stew.

We see the teabag stuck to the mug,
but where are we going to bin it?
Do we need an epic poem, a poem
with economics in it?

How do we turn the charts and graphs
into marches after we say
that the rate you skim from stocks and rocks
outbubbles returns on pay?

How are we going to douse the loans
the dragons pretend to have lent us?
How can we spark agreement among
so many dissenting dissenters?

And which is worse on Middle Earth,
the ring wars ever acuter:
living in fantasies of the past
or fantasies of the future?

Is there a way that we can ensure
that everyone nibbles their share
without the canteen reinstating
Cromwell, Stalin, Robespierre?

How can we stop a pilot from locking
the cabin and crashing the flight?
And once we land, how long will it take
to restore production of Marmite?

Whether or not what's wrong is a plan
or a fluke, we have to foil it:
it seems we know that we need to go,
but not the route to the toilet."

"The corridor's dark, and you've evolved
to believe your parents are right
when they tell you hobbits just aren't up
to unassisted flight.

You'll need good telescopes, Frodo, to see
the wavelengths of the wealth,
its actual size distorted by
its distance to the self.

In any event, I would suggest
· that trade be fair not free:
  let Africans tariff as we once did
  all stuff from across the sea.

· Phase corporate tax out for Meidner levies
  where profits are taxed in shares
  which go to elected wage-earner funds,
  to the locals, that might be fair.

· A one-off tax on wealth to chop
  what's called the "public debt"
  that we've got because we cropped the rates
  on what inheritors get.

· Where there's a bank, there's a way: a tax
  on transactions isn't that hard,
  nor on the taxless preachers of taxes,
  e.g. Madame Lagarde.

· But from the microsecond they take
  your tax, you cannot touch it.
  Beginning with district councils try
  a participatory budget –

  a session a year is not too much
  to vote on what should get more:
  repainting the bogs at the local school
  or the council chamber door.

Send the message out by every modem,
by every wifi router –
read what you can, then ride your buggy,
bike or mobility scooter!

The brass band waltzes Shostakovich,
the Attac demo car
is often best to follow for
a burst of Jean-Michel Jarre.

Among the cycles, prams and bands
you can learn to juggle the factors,
to flutter green flags and thump pink drums,
then storm the towers with tractors!"

"Sounds good," I said, "it might at least
pizazzle this political stasis.
But before we turn the Shire upside down,
what is its theoretical basis?"

"$h = \frac{d}{s}$
where d
is democracy (mental liquidity),
h is total hobbit happiness,
and s represents stupidity."

XXII.

Our hero returns to Luton Airport bearing said yeast extract

Hometime. The clouds as dark as Golgotha,
my coach bumped into the light
of hilltop-glittering Luton, Paradise
Takeaway now to our right,

the roadside shrine no bus route stops at,
my ears not yet under pressure
as we lost the Lost Sock Launderette,
Aldi and Galaxy Leisure,

and like a procession of cases shuffling
into an X-ray machine,
the traffic trailed its way towards
the airport on forty screens

that Plato's digital guardians gaze at.
In the halls of the airspace kings,
calling and clearing, the staff in waistcoats
were waiting to stare through our things

on their twelve-hour shifts, where one once smiled
as she told me I could redon
my unbuckled belt: "We get two days off,
and then it's six days on."

As if it were Christmas again, we queued
in our buzzing lanes for Santa,
in the cordon maze, with a gaze of boredom,
adjusting a reindeer antler

and waiting to slide our wrapped-up gifts
into magic chests, while elves
were checking with certain girls and boys
if they'd behaved themselves,

what they were wearing, had they been good,
and what would they do in Morocco?
Some got to see the man who'd pat them
down in his curtained grotto.

My backpack a jumbo Christmas hamper
of Fourth Doctor DVDs,
there was genuine Cheddar among my clothes
that could do with ninety degrees.

Life is a queue if the queue's for bread
and not for an Alpine chairlift.
Some things are scarce, and I was in charge
of an urgent Berlin Airlift,

concerned the perfect, salty sludge
in my squeezy plastic jar might
count as liquid, airdrop relief
for the lack of affordable Marmite

mid-Brandenburg. I cornered an elf:
"Is Marmite permitted on board?
Surely something can't be liquid
if it can't be poured?"

"'Fraid not, sir," he tilted his head,
revealing a notice on rabies,
"the other day I had to take
a jar from off Steve Davis..."

If only Steve had been behind me
with his champion snooker cue,
he could have ambled about that hall a bit
and deduced the best way through

all packs at every possible angle,
then keeping one eye on that jar
retracted the cue through thumb and finger
like a javelin pulled back far

and whacked that curved black form
with a collider's power, let loose
that particle, all the way up and out
through Luton Departures' roof

and across the branflake fields of East Anglia,
the Adnams-dark North Sea,
electron spun from its orbit,
planetary escapee,

the dark matter that's vital to life,
an isotope, unstable –
and potted it for seven points
upon my breakfast table...

Imagine the close-up, and catch my cry
from the theatre – "I'm going to miss you..." –
and the elf with the ID necklace's commentary:
"You can't take the Marmite with you..."

XXIII.

He awaits his flight home

I lapped a Twix of policemen and looped
the Lady of Passport Control,
as a Quality Street of travellers shifted
in its box, like a startled shoal,

and I strolled along the glossy cliffs
where students of twenty nations
were browsing menus, googling for seats,
masters of non-communication.

+++ *The strange no longer strange* (I read)
although that's strange, I know +++
Another past goes by, one where
you stayed and didn't go +++

I wandered alone about the lounge,
a kerosene translocal
in the infoflow, the worldwide ebb,
one more global yokel.

Our gull not just yet gliding over
a cliff, its Word-white face,
I looked at channels and checked on Maps –
yes, Plato's Cave's a place –

and watched the national nature, drones
filming the watery border
in one collective selfie-taking
personality disorder.

Our plane due now to soon become
one more of the radar blips,
just like the riders lining up
below at Utopia Chips,

and Jenny and Jamie and Janice and Jay,
our valkyries today,
would be passing through with mead and ale
and an opera of options to pay.

The tarmac crew tapped on a switch
in our one-hour time machine
and powered up. I flipped and flipped
through the in-flight magazine:

THE FUTURE once was what we knew
no species ever spies on.
But radio telescopes combined
have found an event horizon.

Beside me, a solemn young man with dreads
and a baggy hat leant back
with Malcolm X and a snap of a double
egg and tomato snack.

Outside, the wind sock billowed. I hoped
our turbines wouldn't incinerate
any gust of pigeons upon its approach.
Our flight was full and late.

Out in the humming, tarmac dark,
wedged in the waiting line
of lights, I watched more runway blips
taxiing out in time.

Notes, sources and acknowledgements

The prefaratory quote from Heinrich Heine is the author's translation.

The 'oval window' (section I): cf. *Play School*, BBC TV, 1964–1988, 'Let's look through the round window'.

Section II includes an executive summary of a poem by Bertolt Brecht translated as 'Ballad of Cortez's men' in Tom Kuhn and David Constantine's *Collected Poems of Bertolt Brecht* (Norton, 2019).

Anyone who is acquainted with Tolkien's Middle Earth will immediately recognize that the village of Brill (section VI) was the model for Bree.

The 'book of utopias' in sections IX and XXI is Erik Olin Wright's highly practical *Envisioning Real Utopias* (Verso, 2010).

The story in section XVIII is from Charlie Mayo, 'King's Cross Diary 1952–3', quoted in David Kynaston's *Austerity Britain* (Bloomsbury, 2007). No pigeons were harmed in the making of this poem.

With thanks to Peter Robinson and all at Two Rivers Press, as well as Ben Borek, Chris Jones (University of Utah), Justin Quinn, David Gordon Smith and, as ever, Sabine Heurs for making this book, hopefully, a bit more *Paradiso* than *Inferno*.

Two Rivers Press has been publishing in and about Reading
since 1994. Founded by the artist Peter Hay (1951–2003),
the press continues to delight readers, local and further afield,
with its varied list of individually designed,
thought-provoking books.